SILLY JOKES FOR KIDS

LAUGH OUT LOUD JOKES FOR KIDS

Copyright © 2017 SillY JOKES FOR KIDS
All rights reserved. This book or any portion thereof
may not be reproduced or used in any manner whatsoever
without the express written permission of the publisher
except for the use of brief quotations in a book review.
Printed Worldwide
First Printing, 2017
ISBN : 1547012315

1.   Why is 6 afraid of 7?

Answer: Because 7 8 9.

---

2.   Why did the chicken cross the playground?

Answer: To get to the other slide.

3. Why didn't the skeleton ride the rollercoaster?

Answer: He just didn't have the guts.

4. What do you get when you cross a vampire with a snowman?

Answer: Frostbite.

5.   How do you make a tissue dance?

Answer: You have to put a little boogie in it.

---

6.   What cleans to bottom of the ocean?

Answer: A mermaid.

7. **Why do bees have sticky hair?**

Answer: Because they style it with a honeycomb.

---

8. **What would you call a pig that knows karate?**

Answer: Pork-Chop.

9.   What does a robotical frog say?

Answer: Rib-bot.

---

10.   Why did the old man run around on his bed?

Answer: He was trying to catch up on his sleep.

11.   Why do cows have to wear bells?

Answer: Because their horns do not work.

12.   How did the crafty barber win a race?

Answer: He knew a short cut.

13.   What did the snail say when he was riding on a turtle's back?

Answer: WEEEEEEEEEE!!

14.   Knock Knock.
Who's there?

Boo.

Boo who?

Please stop crying, it's just a joke.

15. *Knock Knock.*

Who's there?

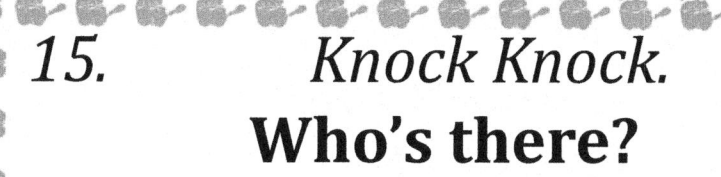

Nobody.

Nobody who?

(SILENCE)

---

16. *Knock Knock.*

Who's there?

Cow's say.

Cow's say who?

No, cow's say moo.

17.   *Knock Knock.*
Who's there?

Tank.

Tank who?

You're welcome.

---

18.   *Knock Knock.*
Who's there?

Owls say.

Owls say who?

Yes, you would be correct.

19. *Knock Knock.*
Who's there?

Little old lady.

Little old lady who?

Awesome, I didn't know that you could yodel.

20. **Why did half of a chicken cross a road?**

Answer: To find his other side.

21. Where do cows go on a Saturday night?

Answer: To the mooooovies.

22. What is brown and sticky?

Answer: A stick.

23. What is mom and dad's favorite ride at the city fair?

Answer: The married go round.

---

24. Where do sheep go to get their wool cut?

Answer: To the baa-bers.

25.   Where do library books go to get their sleep?

Answer: Under the covers.

26.   Why can't a bicycle stand up on its own?

Answer: Because it's just two tired.

27. What do you call a noodle that is fake?

Answer: An impasta.

28. What would you call an alligator in a vest?

Answer: An investigator.

29.   What is the difference between a guitar and a fish?

Answer: You can't Tuna Fish.

30.   What happens if you eat yeast and shoe polish?

Answer: You will rise and shine in the morning.

31.   What do you call a cow with no legs?

Answer: Ground beef.

---

32.   What do you call a cow that is pampered every day?

Answer: Spoiled milk.

33. **What gets wetter the more it dries?**

Answer: A towel

34. **What do lawyers wear to work?**

Answer: Lawsuits.

35. What did one pencil say to the other pencil?

Answer: You look sharp.

---

36. What did the bacon say to the attractive lettuce?

Answer: Lettuce get together for a movie.

37.   What is the smartest part of the eye?

Answer: The pupil.

---

38.   What do you make if you cross an elephant with a fish?

Answer: Swimming trunks.

39.   Why was the picture arrested?

Answer: It was framed.

40.   Who can make a living by driving their customers away?

Answer: A taxi driver.

41. What would you call a baby monkey?

Answer: Just a chimp off of the old block.

---

42. What did the dog do when it swallowed a fire fly?

Answer: It barked with delight.

43.   How do you shoot a killer bee?

Answer: With a bee bee gun.

44.   Why do frogs stay so happy?

Answer: They just eat whatever is bugging them.

45. *Knock Knock.*
Who's there?
Will.

Will who?

Will who let me in, it is pouring rain out here.

---

46. Why did the computer go to the doctor?

Answer: It was scared that it had a virus.

47.   Why did the cookie go to the doctor?

Answer: It was feeling kind of crumby.

---

48.   What is the tallest building in the world?

Answer: The library, it has the most stories.

49. **What would you call a sleeping bull?**

Answer: A bull-dozer.

50. *Knock Knock.*
Who's there?

Barbie.
Barbie who?

Barbie Q.

51.   What stays in the corner, yet travels all over the world?

Answer: A stamp.

52.   What do you get when you cross a duck with a cow?

Answer: Milk and quackers.

53.   What do you call a belt that has a watch on it?

Answer: A waist of time.

54.   Why is England the wettest country?

Answer: Because the Queen has reigned there for over 3 years.

55.   Why do fish live in salt water?

Answer: Because pepper tends to make them sneeze.

56.   Why did the banana go to the doctor?

Answer: It just wasn't peeling well.

57.   What bow can never be tied?

Answer: A rainbow.

---

58.   What is always the best day to go to the beach

Answer: Sunday.

59.   Why did the burglar hide his money in the freezer?

Answer: He had cold, hard cash.

---

60.   Knock Knock.
Who's there?

Figs.
Figs who?

Figs the doorbell, it doesn't work.

61.   Where did the computer go to dance?

Answer: The disc-o.

---

62.   What is the best season to jump on a trampoline?

Answer: Spring time.

63. What has one head, one foot, and four legs?

Answer: A bed.

---

64. What is a big difference between a train and a school teacher?

Answer: One says spit out your gum, while the other says chew, chew, chew.

65. Why was a man looking for food on his best friend?

Answer: Because he said dinner was on him.

66. Why did the little birdie go to the doctor?

Answer: To get his tweetment.

67.   What do you call someone who is afraid of Santa?

Answer: Claustrophobic.

---

68.   What sound do porcupines make when they kiss?

Answer: Ouch.

69.   What is brown that has one head, one tail, and no legs?

Answer: A penny.

---

70.   *Knock Knock.*
Who's there?

Kiwi.
Kiwi who?

Kiwi go to the movies?

71.   How do you get fired from making calendars?

Answer: You leave off some dates.

---

72.   Did you hear the joke about roofs?

Answer: Never mind, it would go over your head.

73.   Why didn't the skeleton go to the dance?

Answer: He had no body to go with.

74.   What do prisoners use to call each other?

Answer: Cell phones.

75.   Why are pirates called pirates?

Answer: Because they just arrrrrrr.

---

76.   How do crazy people go through a crowded forest?

Answer: They take the psycho path.

77.   Where do snowmen keep their money?

Answer: In snow banks.

78.   What did the tiny mountain say to the big mountain?

Answer: Hello there, Cliff.

79.   What washes up on tiny beaches?

Answer: Microwaves.

---

80.   Knock Knock.
Who's there?

Lettuce.
Lettuce who?

Lettuce in, it is freezing out here.

81.   What goes through every town but never moves?

Answer: The road.

---

82.   Why was there lightning and thunder in the lab?

Answer: The scientists were just brainstorming.

83.   What would you call a funny mountain?

Answer: Hill-arious.

---

84.   What did Winnie the Pooh say to his agent?

Answer: Show me the honey!

85.   What did one candle say to the other candle?

Answer: As dim as it is, I am going out tonight.

---

86.   Why couldn't the pirate play cards?

Answer: He was sitting on the deck.

87.   How do you make an octopus laugh?

Answer: With ten-ticles.

88.   What did the gamer say when he lost a match on the Wii?

Answer: I want a Wii-match.

89.   Why do traffic lights turn red?
Answer: Because they have to change in the middle of the street.

90.   Knock Knock.
Who's there?

Turnip.
Turnip who?

Turnip the volume, it's time to dance!

91.   What did one elevator say to the other elevator?

Answer: I think I am coming down with something.

---

92.   What never asks questions but gets a lot of answers?

Answer: A telephone.

93.   Why can't your nose be 12 inches long?

Answer: Because then it would be a foot.

---

94.   What starts with a P, ends with an E, and has a million letters in it?

Answer: A post office.

95. What did the blanket say to the nervous bed?

Answer: Don't worry, I've got you covered.

96. What has four wheels and flies?

Answer: A garbage truck.

97. How many books can you fit in an empty back pack?

Answer: Only one, after that it's not empty anymore.

---

98. Why should you take a pencil to your bedroom?

Answer: To draw the curtains.

99.   What kind of floor is in a day care?

Answer: Infant-tile.

100.   *Knock Knock.*
Who's there?

Ice cream.
Ice cream who?

Ice cream if you won't let me in.

101. What kind of button won't unbutton?

Answer: A bellybutton.

102. What did the triangle say to the circle?

Answer: You are completely pointless.

103. Why don't seagulls fly over the bay?

Answer: Because then they would be called bagels.

104. What dog can keep the best time?

Answer: A watch dog.

105. What noise did the grape make when it was stepped on?

Answer: It just let out a little wine.

106. Why did the tomato turn red?

Answer: It saw the salad dressing.

107.   What did the judge say when the skunk walked in to the court room?

Answer: Odor in the court.

108.   What did the fish say when it slammed into the wall?

Answer: Dam!

109. Why won't skeletons fight each other?

Answer: They don't have the guts.

110. *Knock Knock.*
Who's there?
Police.
Police who?

Police, can I come in?

111. What did the janitor say when he jumped out of the closet?

Answer: Supplies!

112. What did the traffic light say to the car?

Answer: Don't look, I'm changing.

113. Why was the student's report card wet?

Answer: It was below C level.

114. What do you call cheese that isn't yours?

Answer: Nacho cheese.

115.   How do you find a Princess?

Answer: You follow the foot Prince.

---

116.   What streets do ghosts haunt?

Answer: Dead ends.

117. What did one penny say to the other penny?

Answer: We make perfect cents.

---

118. What kind of music are balloons afraid of?

Answer: Pop music

119.   Why did the robber take a bath?

Answer: He wanted to make sure he made a clean get away.

---

120.   *Knock Knock.*
Who's there?

Water.
Water who?

Water you doing, this is my house.

121.   Why did the one handed man cross the road?

Answer: To get to the second hand shop.

---

122.   What do you get when you cross a fridge with a radio?

Answer: Really cool music.

123. What goes up when rain comes down?

Answer: Umbrellas.

---

124. Why did the little boy tip toe past the medicine cabinet?

Answer: He didn't want to wake the sleeping pills.

125. What did the judge say to the dentist?

Answer: Do you swear to pull the tooth, the whole tooth, and nothing but the tooth.

126. Why did the belt go to jail?

Answer: It held up a pair of pants.

127.　What did the stamp say to the envelope?

Answer: If you stick with me, we will go places.

128.　What kind of lights did Noah use on the Ark?

Answer: Flood lights.

129.   Why don't you see giraffes in elementary school?

Answer: Because they are all in high school.

---

130. Knock Knock.
Who's there?

Goat.
Goat who?

Goat to the door and let me in.

131.   What month do soldiers like the most?

Answer: The month of March.

---

132.   What did the painter say to the wall?

Answer: One more crack like that and I will plaster you.

133. Why did the computer break up with the internet?

Answer: There just wasn't a connection.

134. Why do golfers wear two pair of pants?

Answer: In case they get a hole in one.

135. Why can't you take a nap during a race?

Answer: If you snooze, you lose.

---

136. What is the longest word in the dictionary?

Answer: Smiles. There is a mile between each s.

137.   Why did the man put a clock under his desk?

Answer: He wanted to work over time.

---

138.   What do you call a book that is about the brain?

Answer: A mind reader.

139. When do you stop at green and go at red?

Answer: When you are eating a watermelon.

---

140. *Knock Knock.*
Who's there?

Leaf.
Leaf who?

Leaf me alone, I don't want to talk.

141.   How did the farmer mend his pants?

Answer: With cabbage patches.

142.   How do you fix a broken tomato?

Answer: With tomato paste.

143. Why did the man lose his job at the orange juice factory?

Answer: He couldn't concentrate.

---

144. Why did the baby strawberry cry?

Answer: His parents were in a jam.

145. What did the hamburger name his daughter?

Answer: Patty.

146. What kind of egg did the bad chicken lay?

Answer: A deviled egg.

147. What do you call a guy who never farts in public?

Answer: A private tutor.

---

148. What can you serve but never eat?

Answer: A volleyball.

149. What kind of shoes do spies wear?

Answer: Sneakers.

---

150. What do you call a bear with no socks on?

Answer: Bear foot.

Which of these awesome amimals can you find ?

```
F T B U S B Y O J B D D X P U
Z U Q W K W T B B Y F T P T Z
V R B Z H D E L E P H A N T I
Q T A L K D Q D S A T K X K E
F L T L R Q F Z Z L H B P A W
I E L M G I B E K L L U E N M
S H E Y O R M S Q I Z S F G Z
H H M W R C G C F G E G I A M
H P I G I D J G U A R I B R M
W G W K L U A Y U T J R A O H
L I O N L O E U W O O A N O E
F X M U A H F G F R W F T R U
Q M Q F D B F R O Z T F J G F
K H B Z P H V C R A T E S R X
O K K U E K K M X K T T E O G
```

77

Can you find any yummy food in this word search?

K	R	E	U	R	C	U	F	J	F
O	W	U	H	M	D	Q	T	K	V
Z	F	H	E	A	N	K	H	B	C
N	B	A	E	H	F	I	S	H	P
R	T	R	C	A	K	E	E	L	I
K	B	Q	K	M	T	E	M	C	Z
A	S	U	V	L	S	P	O	N	Z
N	U	E	V	E	I	R	L	L	A
Y	S	G	G	E	F	M	T	N	Y
Q	R	I	R	W	N	P	E	A	S

Can you find all the planets in the solar system?

I	I	Q	S	U	N	A	R	U	O
O	B	I	A	J	J	O	B	F	H
M	E	R	C	U	R	Y	F	J	C
V	E	Q	Z	L	Z	V	U	F	Q
E	Y	N	K	S	U	P	P	S	D
N	R	H	U	A	I	S	W	S	W
U	D	O	H	T	R	A	E	R	O
S	O	Y	E	U	P	P	X	A	Y
Y	F	R	G	R	K	E	J	M	A
Z	Z	I	E	N	F	P	N	U	Q

MARS   JUPITER   URANUS
NEPTUNE   VENUS   EARTH
SATURN   MERCURY

Can you find these Jungle animals?

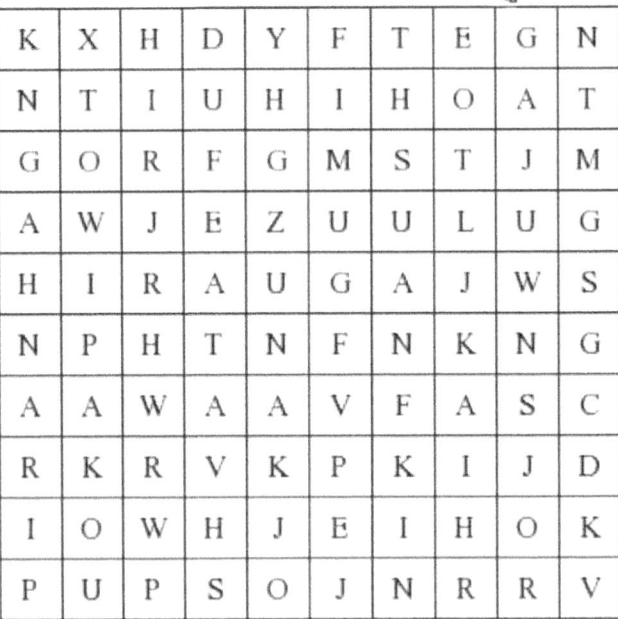

K	X	H	D	Y	F	T	E	G	N
N	T	I	U	H	I	H	O	A	T
G	O	R	F	G	M	S	T	J	M
A	W	J	E	Z	U	U	L	U	G
H	I	R	A	U	G	A	J	W	S
N	P	H	T	N	F	N	K	N	G
A	A	W	A	A	V	F	A	S	C
R	K	R	V	K	P	K	I	J	D
I	O	W	H	J	E	I	H	O	K
P	U	P	S	O	J	N	R	R	V

JAGUAR
SNAKE
PIRANHA
OKAPI
TIGER
ORANGUTAN
FROG
TAPIR

Can you find the vegetables?

G	O	D	N	D	H	M	K	R	S
A	C	A	R	R	O	T	Y	E	W
R	E	G	G	P	L	A	N	T	P
L	K	E	Q	V	E	W	E	P	Z
I	J	C	U	C	U	M	B	E	R
C	D	Y	J	M	D	N	D	O	V
X	D	A	K	I	R	P	A	P	Y
B	A	L	T	O	M	A	T	O	S
U	F	X	N	O	I	N	O	J	A
Z	O	Q	X	C	L	F	K	A	N

Winter fun word search

K	E	E	R	T	L	F	Y	W	M
H	E	B	C	U	J	O	O	I	A
Z	F	L	O	D	U	R	S	N	E
J	A	T	N	A	S	N	B	T	G
F	N	A	M	W	O	N	S	E	D
X	Y	D	C	W	D	S	G	R	E
W	Y	Q	B	T	B	M	N	T	L
E	B	A	Y	E	K	R	U	T	S
U	L	R	Z	F	Y	L	E	C	K
L	O	K	P	H	X	H	K	Y	P

SNOWMAN
TREE
SNOWBALL
WINTER
SLEDGE
RUDOLF
SANTA
TURKEY

Can you find the fruit?

M	V	Y	Z	Z	I	H	B	K	U
F	A	F	L	N	U	T	G	A	A
J	N	E	L	M	M	F	D	H	L
V	A	Y	A	P	A	P	V	C	T
E	N	P	Z	D	N	N	X	W	I
E	A	R	P	E	O	P	G	W	A
G	B	F	Y	L	M	W	I	O	P
X	P	D	Z	X	E	K	X	F	Z
A	L	G	G	C	L	A	S	Q	G
S	O	R	A	N	G	E	W	E	M

APPLE
ORANGE
KIWI
BANANA
PAPAYA
MANGO
LEMON

Made in the USA
Middletown, DE
25 March 2022